WHO IS HUSSAIN?

WHO IS HUSSAIN?

Second Edition

Haj Dr. Mehdi Saeed Hazari

I.M.A.M.

IMAM MAHDI ASSOCIATION OF MARJAEYA

Imam Mahdi Association of Marjaeya, Dearborn, MI
48124, www.imam-us.org

© 2016 by Imam Mahdi Association of Marjaeya

All rights reserved. Published 2016. Second printing
2019.

Printed in the United States of America.

ISBN: 978-0-9862951-9-5

Contents

I.M.A.M.'s Foreword

Many personalities from different nations and in different periods of time have appeared and distinguished themselves in the history of humankind. The status of these figures has risen beyond their nations, people, and geographic borders so that they are universally recognized and distinguished as sensations in their respective realms.

However, there are some who stand out even among those eminent figures. These individuals were able to not only establish balance between the body and the soul, the physical and the metaphysical, the sensory and the extrasensory, but also changed the course of humanity in such a positive way that they became exemplars for all times to come. These distinguished figures are the prophets, the messengers, and their legatees—those who were chosen by God Almighty to perform acts that would become an everlasting beacon of guidance for humanity. Furthermore, each of the divinely chosen prophets (e.g., Noah,

i

Abraham, Moses, Jesus, and Muhammad) distinguished themselves from their counterparts with specific characteristics and feats of faith, patience, and courage.

As such, the entire historical legacy of the divine message, as transmitted by all the prophets and messengers, reached its peak and completion with the seal of the prophets, Prophet Muhammad, who eventually placed this legacy in the hands of Hussain, his grandson, who ensured the continuation of the religion. For the Prophet announced in his famous and authentic tradition, "Hussain is of me and I am of Hussain." The Prophet's expression was significant and noteworthy for several reasons—the most important of which is "My message and divine mission will not continue except through Hussain."

Surely, Hussain, the grandson of Prophet Muhammad and the inheritor of the prophetic message, gave all that he owned in the way of God Almighty in a manner that is historically unmatched. He became the means through which God Almighty would eternally preserve divine religion—through the sacrifice of Hussain's pure blood in the Battle of Karbala.

The great feat of Hussain and the tragedy of Karbala is commemorated annually throughout the world. The memorials increase in scale and attendance every year and in a fashion that has become noticeable on a global scale. This has not occurred due to planning by certain organizations but from the sincere faith and devotion of each of Hussain's followers. Each year the commemorations culminate in the miraculous gathering of millions on the fortieth day after his martyrdom (known as Arbaeen). It is on that day that approximately twenty million visitors make a pilgrimage to his holy shrine, walking tens and hundreds of miles to reach Karbala. Amongst them are hundreds of thousands of people from different countries around the world. The visitors of Hussain are diverse, representing different sects, ethnicities, languages, and nationalities; men and women; young and old. What brings them together is nothing other than the love of Hussain.

This booklet is a humble attempt to spread this crucially important message and miracle. Indeed, the aim is that those who have not heard of Hussain will get to know about him, and those who have heard of him but do not know who he was or what he stood for will learn about the magnificence of his character. We see this as the duty of those who love Hussain, for it is the truth, and the truth should not be kept from anyone.

This new edition of the booklet has been reviewed and revised by the respected Haj Dr. Mehdi Hazari. We hope that this blessed work will reach its purpose. I would like to thank the entire I.M.A.M. publication team who worked very hard to provide the best of what could be offered to our respected readers. We ask God Almighty to accept this work and that it will intercede for us on the Day of Judgment.

Sayyid M. B. Kashmiri
Jurist Representative
I.M.A.M.

Acknowledgements

This book is dedicated to all the righteous men and women who have struggled for justice, equity, and the preservation of human rights and dignity over the course of history. To us, the followers of Prophet Muhammad and his Holy Household, Hussain and all those who were martyred alongside him in Karbala represent the pinnacle of that struggle.

The original content for this book, some of which is contained herein, was written by Shaykh Aous Asfar, whose thorough research, particularly in terms of evidence from the Holy Quran and traditions, as well as tireless and sincere efforts, cannot be acknowledged with words. It is only through the hard work and dedication of such an individual that this book is possible.

As such, a revision of the first edition was necessary so the history of Karbala could be presented in a more comprehensive manner to a Western audience of peoples from other religions as well as Muslims who are not familiar with Hussain. To achieve this, additional historical background and hagiographical information are now provided so the respected reader can fully appreciate the scope of Karbala, its causes, and its ramifications. In addition, the original writing style was changed toward a more active form with the intention of creating an image or scene in the mind of the lay reader. This is an important experiential point because most Shia Muslims relate to Karbala, and lament it as if they were present with Hussain.

Furthermore, minor organizational changes (e.g., moving sections) and deletion of redundant parts were made to help with the flow of events. Finally, although the structure, research, and references remain unchanged, most of the book has been rewritten and expanded so that the reader will be able to relate to the cause of Hussain and understand the timelessness and universality of its relevance.

Special thanks are also due to everyone involved in making this project possible, especially I.M.A.M., Sayyid Muhammad Baqir Kashmiri, and Haj Mustafa

S. Hassan for their continued support of important educational publications.

Introduction

Every Muslim, regardless of race, background, ethnicity, sect, or social status, considers the Holy Quran to be the immutable word of God Almighty that contains and describes every aspect of Islam. It is the source that is consulted first and foremost when matters of any significance related to the religion of Islam need clarification or explanation. As such, it must be interpreted and applied based on the legitimate dictates of Islam and with the proper context, especially given the wicked intentions of those who seek to corrupt its meaning in order to achieve their own personal goals. In addition, every Muslim regards the authentic traditions (i.e., the words, actions, and silent assertions), or the *sunnah*, of Prophet Muhammad to be a secondary source of Islamic verities which specifically demonstrate his human actions and provide a code of practice and a model of perfect behavior. Thus, this booklet uses the above-mentioned sources as both a reference and a measure of authenticity.

Chapter 1

Hypocrites Disguised as Muslims Then and Now

After the death of Prophet Muhammad in 632 CE, various factions were vying for power and control of the Muslim nation. One family, the Umayyads, used illicit means to secure influence and eventually wield power over Muslims. The Umayyads were driven by greed, self-interest, and a decades-old grudge against the family of Prophet Muhammad. Their illegitimate regime was deeply rooted in paganism and gave no importance to justice or equity. Prior to Islam, they were tribal patriarchs who ruled Arabia through feuds, archaic customs, and murder. They were very wealthy and accrued their wealth through dishonesty, coercion, and blackmail. Much to their distress, Islam had come to rid the world of their paganism, immorality, and thievery.

During his life, as the Prophet gained supporters and built a core of strong, loyal followers, he was able to seize control of Mecca. Though the Umayyads were starkly against him and the egalitarian message of Islam, they realized that the only way they were going to preserve what was left of their dwindling influence in the growing Islamic nation was by feigning to accept Islam. They would bide their time until an opportune moment when they could seize back power from the Prophet. After the death of the Prophet, they usurped the caliphate (highest position of leadership after the Prophet) from its rightfully appointed leader and started to fashion the religion according to their own desires.

After examining some of the historical facts presented by notable scholars from all of the major sects of Islam, it becomes blatantly clear that the actions of hostility that resulted in the assassination of the Prophet's grandson Hussain, his brother Hasan, and his father Ali were acts of revenge and greed for power that were carried out by hypocrites disguised as Muslims. There was no intention of spreading the peaceful ethos of Islam, which seeks dignity for every human being. Yazid, son of

Muawiyah (an Umayyad), himself admitted this fact, and his illegitimate installment as leader incriminates his father, Muawiyah, and his grandfather, Abu Sufyan. This lineage of Umayyads continued to reign until they were overthrown and replaced by the Abbasids who would gain power and retain it by the same nefarious means—their goals were no different!

Indeed, it is this syndicate of criminals who hijacked the religion of Islam to ensure that power remained in their clutches. Their form of Islam was so deviant that it led them to murder the most beloved grandsons of the Prophet of God. When the Prophet himself declares them transgressors, invokes God's curse upon them, and prays to the Almighty that they will not have divine grace, then they are as far as one can possibly be from Islam. Furthermore, they sanctioned the introduction of false elements and practices, many of which persist today, into the religion of Islam and moved people away from the deep connection that it creates for humanity with their creator.

3

These deviants showed no respect for human life. Anyone who stood in their way was executed, even the messenger of Caesar. They demonstrated that their goals and objectives were not founded on justice and fairness but on tyranny, persecution, and usurpation by any means necessary. Not even the women and children of the Prophet were spared from their evil ways. Unfortunately, some Muslims during that time sought to practice Islam the way the Umayyads did—with the same egomaniacal goals and greed for wealth. They used the rise of the Umayyads as their opportunity to advance themselves. This included control of regional wealth; consolidation of power and money among the few, which their political strategies would ensure for years to come; and ruling through despotism, intimidation, and bloodshed. They would essentially create their own version of Islam using corrupt scholars and hired mercenaries.

The ruthless regime of the Umayyads is an exact reflection of what we see today in the Middle East from those imposters who disguise themselves in the garb of a Muslim but perpetrate heinous criminal acts—execution, decapitation, raping of women, and killing of the innocent. For this reason, Hussain's sacrifice and courageous stand resonates boldly today to remind us that we cannot silently accept injustice and the terrorizing of any people.

The Islam we see portrayed today by many so-called Muslim leaders and apparent zealots is the same version of Islam that the Umayyads innovated. It is one that is in direct contradiction to the teachings of the Holy Quran and the sunnah of the Holy Prophet, which direct people to equity, morality, tolerance, and peaceful coexistence with others. God states in the Holy Quran, "People, We have created you all male and female and have made you nations and tribes so that you would recognize each other. The most honorable among you in the sight of God is the most pious of you." (49:13), "If they (the unbelievers) propose peace, accept it and trust in God." (8:61), and "God does not forbid you to deal kindly and justly with those who did not fight against you about the religion nor did they expel you from your homes. God does not love the unjust people." (60:8)

The struggle of Hussain at Karbala was to preserve this very message. In doing so, he reminded people that the so-called Islam of the Umayyads was nothing more than a personal manifesto aimed at promoting themselves and quashing anyone who resisted. Hussain resisted; and by giving the ultimate sacrifice, he not only awakened the hearts of Muslims who began to question the legitimacy of the Umayyad regime, he also preserved the religion by distinguishing it from the deviant, innovated, extremist form of Islam advocated by the Umayyads. Finally, the legacy of Hussain is not restricted to Muslims but reminds every person, particularly today, that injustice and tyranny cannot be tolerated and that each one of us can cause tangible and long-lasting change. Furthermore, Hussain demonstrated that even a small group of faithful and steadfast individuals can preserve the true message of a religion, movement, or cause from the extremist ideology of those who seek to hijack and pervert it.

It is up to the discerning reader to realize the danger that such despots and regimes, who seek to enslave the free and kill the innocent for money and power, pose to the free people of the world. In addition, one must distinguish extremist ideology from the real message of any religion and realize that with the right motivation, any person can distort the true meaning of religious doctrine to make it appear exactly the opposite of what it truly is. We ask God Almighty to guide us all to His truth and inspire us to be just, merciful, and tolerant of each other like all the great personalities whom He chose as an example to humanity.

Chapter 2
What Is Karbala?

The event of Karbala (also known as the Battle of Karbala) took place on the tenth of Muharram, which is the first month of the Islamic calendar, 61 AH (October 680 CE) in Karbala, a barren desert region in present-day Iraq. The battle took place between (1) Hussain, the grandson of Prophet Muhammad and the rightful leader of the Muslim nation, and his small band of supporters and (2) a large military force from the army of Yazid son of Muawiyah who was the self-proclaimed caliph in Damascus, Syria, and leader of the Umayyad dynasty. This conflict was the result of many years of corruption, tyranny, and oppression at the hands of the Umayyads who were determined to desecrate Islam and its sanctity to serve their own interests. As such, Hussain refused to pledge allegiance to such a despot and so left the city of his grandfather (Medina) with his womenfolk and children to rally support in Kufa, Iraq (whose residents had written him thousands of letters of support), and to resist the growing corruption of Yazid. However, after being abandoned by most of his so-called supporters who succumbed to bribery and intimidation, Hussain was forced to take a stand with seventy-three loyal companions and members of his family to preserve the religion of his grandfather. This action resulted in the martyrdom of Hussain and all his supporters and the capture, imprisonment, and terrorization of his womenfolk and children. Since then, Muslims around the world, especially Shia Muslims, commemorate this tragic event in Muharram and especially on the Day of Ashura, the tenth, by not only recalling the valor and courage of Hussain and his supporters but also their devotion to God and resolve to defend justice and equity. It is with tears and lamentation that his supporters keep this universal message alive.

Chapter 3

Who Is Hussain?

Lineage: The family of Hashim (tribe of Quraysh)

Father: Ali son of Abu Talib, the cousin of Prophet Muhammad and the first imam[1]

Mother: Lady Fatimah al-Zahra (Fatimah, the splendid one), the daughter of Prophet Muhammad and wife of Ali

Grandfather: Prophet Muhammad

Hussain's upbringing

Hussain was born in Medina, which is in present-day Saudi Arabia, in 626 CE (4 AH). He and his older brother Hasan (the second imam) were named by their grandfather Muhammad, the prophet of Islam,

---

1. *Imam* generally means a leader or guide. Shia Muslims consider the Imams, who are the twelve successive leaders and legatees of Islam from the family of Prophet Muhammad, to be divinely chosen. This booklet will use the term in the latter sense.

and raised under his guidance and love. He witnessed all the challenges and difficulties faced by Muslims in the early post-migration[2] days of Islam and learned from his grandfather how to deal with adversity and foster unity and growth in the Muslim community. This is particularly relevant given that the Muslim community at that time was under constant assault from groups like the pagan idol worshippers and various others, including even from so-called Muslims who had only accepted Islam because it served a personal, tribal, or political agenda. Consequently, this latter group would eventually usurp the rights of the family of the Prophet (e.g., illegally confiscating the inherited land of Fatimah, which was given to her by her father) and foment hostility against them and spill their blood.

---

2. The Islamic calendar starts with this migration (*hijra*). It is when Prophet Muhammad emigrated from his hometown of Mecca to Medina after thirteen years of delivering the message of Islam to the pagans of the region. He left to escape persecution and constant threats on his life and the lives of Muslims. The Islamic calendar is abbreviated with AH (after hijra).

Hussain's relationship with his grandfather the Prophet

Usama son of Zayd, a companion of Prophet Muhammad once said, "I knocked on the door of the Prophet for a need, he was seated with his grandsons and he said, 'These (Hasan and Hussain) are my sons and my daughter's sons. O God, I love them, so [you] love them, and love whoever loves them.'"[3] Prophet Muhammad's use of the phrase "my sons" was not merely symbolic—it accurately described the relationship of the Prophet, who had no sons of his own, to Hasan and Hussain. This love took the form of not only fatherly compassion and kindness but also rearing and education, for the brothers literally grew up in the lap of the Prophet.

Hussain as a significant historical figure not only for Muslims but for all people

Hussain represented the stand of those who would not accept tyranny and injustice, regardless of race,

---

3. *Jami tirmidhi*, "Merits of al-Hasan and al-Hussain," hadith 4144.

religion, or ethnicity. After the death of Prophet Muhammad, the Muslim community became increasingly mired in self-interest, nepotism, and social disparity, which included ethnic prejudice, the hoarding of wealth, and the distortion of religious laws for personal gain. These inequities reached a peak when Yazid was illegitimately appointed caliph by his father and began openly committing injustices, defiling basic human rights, and violating the tenets of Islam.

In reality, Hussain was the person who was most respected by Muslims and the most suitable to assume the caliphate, irrespective of divine appointment. Fully aware of the growing strife in the nation, Hussain had to make very crucial decisions to preserve what his grandfather, father, brother, and many other Muslims had struggled to achieve. Indeed, his indelible impression on humankind exists today because he was not seeking power, nor did he want war or the spilling of blood. Why else would he leave the sanctuary of his grandfather in Medina and ride toward Iraq with his womenfolk and children accompanying him? These were certainly not the actions of a man seeking war. Rather, the state of corruption had become so critical that Hussain refused to acknowledge its perpetrators as legitimate and took a stand. That stand led to his death and forever showed all of humanity that no sacrifice is too great for the preservation of God's truth and justice.

To know Hussain is to know Prophet Muhammad and the Holy Quran

In Islam, Prophet Muhammad's actions and sayings are considered the model of excellent behavior and an example of the best character. This is what is called *sunnah*. As God states in the Holy Quran, "The Messenger of God is certainly a good example." (33:21) God declares that His messenger (Muhammad) does not act of his own accord, "He does not speak out of his own desires. It (whatever he says) is a revelation which has been revealed to him." (53:3–4) And God commands us to obey Him, His prophet, and His imams, "Believers obey God, His Messenger, and your (qualified) leaders." (4:59) And

God states, "Only God, His Messenger, and the true believers who are steadfast in prayer and pay alms, while they bow down during prayer, are your guardians." (5:55)[4]

Through these verses, God establishes the authority of Prophet Muhammad based on the divine will that his every utterance and gesture are a result of His command, and so obedience should be to him (Prophet Muhammad) and his legatees since they are the administrators of God's religion on Earth.

Hence, when God Almighty states on the tongue of His prophet in the Holy Quran, "Say, 'I do not ask you for any payment for my preaching to you except (your) love of (my near) relatives." (42:23), showing them respect and love, pledging allegiance to them, supporting their cause, and upholding their rights is obedience to God and His message. As such, the recognition of Hussain as not only the family of

---

4. The consensus among all Islamic scholars is that this verse is about Hussain's father, Ali.

Prophet Muhammad but also as a legatee is an integral part of this obligation.

Those included in the distinction of kinship and authority

On several occasions, Prophet Muhammad was observed and documented recognizing certain members of his family. On one such occasion, he gathered four of them and himself under a Yemeni cloak in his home—this is known as the tradition of the cloak. On that occasion, Ali, Hasan, Hussain, and Fatimah gathered under the cloak with the Prophet, and God revealed a verse of the Holy Quran in light of the event, saying, "O People of the house, God wants to remove all kinds of uncleanness from you and to purify you thoroughly." (33:33)

Only the People of the Household, those from the lineage of the prophets, and Lady Mary (mother of Jesus) were said to be purified in the Holy Quran, "God chose (and gave distinction to) Adam, Noah, the family of Abraham, and Imran over all the people of the world." (3:33) "'Behold,' the angels told Mary,

'God has chosen you, purified you, and given you distinction over all women.'" (3:42)

Why divine purification is important

God purifies only those whom He divinely appoints as His representatives on Earth. Therefore, divine purification makes these figures extremely important for the salvation of humankind. Why? Because humankind could not possibly trust the morality of a representative of God who erred even once.

Chapter 4

Circumstances That Led to Karbala

Ali's caliphate and death

Between 632 CE (11 AH), which is when Prophet Muhammad died, and 656 CE (35 AH), three men (Abu Bakr son of Abu Quhafa, Umar son of Khattab, and Uthman son of Affan) assumed the caliphate successively. Ali son of Abu Talib, who had grown up under the guidance of Prophet Muhammad and was unmatched in his service to Islam, was overlooked. In 656 CE (35 AH), only after Uthman's death did Ali become caliph and reluctantly so due to his dislike for politics and disinterest in worldly power.

Ali was the only one of the first four caliphs who was born and grew up never having believed or practiced the pagan religions; like Muhammad, he had always been a monotheist. Furthermore, he was the first to pledge support to Muhammad at the advent of his prophetic mission and was thus the first Muslim. In fact, his knowledge and understanding of Islam and its laws, and his ability to deal fairly and compassionately with people, far surpassed any other member of the community. Ali's disdain for worldly politics did not stop him from assisting and guiding the previous three caliphs in upholding the correct principles of Islam—so much so that Umar was heard on numerous occasions saying, "I seek Allah's help in deciding those difficult problems for which Abu al-Hasan [Ali] is not available."[5] Yet, by the time he assumed the caliphate, the Islamic world had devolved into corruption and hoarding of wealth, some of which was at the hands of the Umayyads, and moved away from the true teachings of Islam. Thus, Ali resolved to correct the wrongs that had occurred during the previous twenty-five years.

Ali staunchly upheld justice and fairness to such a degree that his relatives, let alone his enemies, sometimes complained that under him they could not unfairly benefit from their relationship to him

5. Ibn Hajar Makki, *Sawaiq muhriqa*, chapter 3.

and the Prophet. Due to this firm stance, Ali was forced to fight three major battles during his caliphate against groups who were either pursuing personal agendas, sowing dissension and animosity among Muslims, or usurping property and spreading corruption:

- The Battle of the Camel (Jamal) in which Aisha (wife of the Prophet and daughter of the first caliph, Abu Bakr) and some others led an army against Ali in Basra, Iraq, to seek vengeance for what was claimed as the assassination of Uthman. Ali was innocent of these accusations and was only targeted for political reasons.

- The Battle of Siffin, which was fought against Muawiyah son of Abu Sufyan and his army from Damascus. Muawiyah, who was the leader of the Umayyad dynasty, was only a Muslim by name. His unending schemes of bribery, manipulation, and covert assassinations were what forced Ali to battle this evil.

- The Battle of Nahrawan, which was against the Kharijites who fought Ali after being in his ranks, because they believed that he had gone

against God's religion by negotiating a truce
with Muawiyah in the Battle of Siffin

Thus, one can see the turmoil and instability that was arising in the Muslim nation and fully grasp that the reason the Battle of Karbala eventually took place was the stand of those who sought to resist and fight the corruption and greed of the Umayyads and their associates at any cost.

Sadly, five years into his caliphate, Ali son of Abu Talib was assassinated by Ibn Muljim who sought revenge for the Kharijite losses in the Battle of Nahrawan.

Hasan appointed caliph

In 660 CE (40 AH), after the death of Ali, Muslims pledged their allegiance to Hasan (Ali's first-born son and older brother of Hussain), who was the rightful leader by the instruction of the Prophet. His caliphate lasted for almost six months.

Muawiyah ruthlessly challenges Hasan

At that time, Muawiyah was the governor of Damascus (Syria). He was appointed to this position by the second caliph—a move which subsequently led to the re-emergence of the Umayyad family. This power was consolidated to some degree by the third caliph who shared kinship with them. Muawiyah's objective was to gain control of the caliphate (for the Umayyad family) after the assassination of Ali, so he challenged Hasan by bribing and intimidating those with weak faith. He even seduced Hasan's cousin to betray him.

In addition, Muawiyah placed a great deal of pressure on Hasan by ruthlessly killing his supporters (Shia) in a campaign of mass genocide—killing all those who did not disassociate from Ali and engage in the institutionalized practice of cursing him from the pulpit. Muawiyah imprisoned many of the followers of the Holy Household of the Prophet (*Ahl al-Bayt* in Arabic) and demolished many of their homes.

The Treaty of Hasan

After almost six months as caliph and with dwindling support, Hasan wanted to end the bloodshed and decided to sign a truce with Muawiyah under the condition that he abide by its terms, which included the following:

- Rule in accordance with the Holy Quran and the sunnah of the Prophet
- Stop the institutionalized cursing of Ali
- Return all property to its rightful owners
- Rule with justice and equity
- Stop bloodshed
- Release innocent prisoners
- Not appoint anyone caliph after him

Muawiyah usurps the caliphate

Muawiyah agreed to the terms of the treaty at first, but a few days later at the public ceremony for the treaty, he renounced the agreement and said, "I do not agree to this treaty, it is beneath my feet (i.e., it holds no power over me), and I will not abide by any of its terms." Over the next year, he began to usurp the caliphate using the devious tactics he was known for.

Muslims try to revolt against Muawiyah

Many Muslims from Iraq wrote to Hasan requesting a revolution against Muawiyah. But Hasan told them to be patient until the death of Muawiyah. On the other hand, there were not enough sincere supporters with which to revolt, lest a repeat of the Battle of Siffin occur.

Muawiyah assassinates Hasan

In the year 669 CE (49 AH), not willing to give any opportunity to Hasan, Muawiyah bribed Jada, the wife of Hasan, to poison him. Her reward for this crime was to be one thousand dirhams and marriage to Muawiyah's son Yazid. She poisoned Hasan, and he died shortly thereafter. Jada received her monetary reward, but she was denied marriage to Yazid because Muawiyah feared that she would betray his son just as she betrayed Hasan. Muawiyah remained in power until he died in 680 CE (60 AH) but not before solidifying the succession of Yazid as caliph in Damascus.

Chapter 5

Karbala: Hussain's Journey to His Destiny

The Battle of Karbala took place on October 10, 680 CE (Muharram 10, 61 AH)—1,339 years ago.

The prophecy of Karbala

Prophet Muhammad was informed of the tragedy of Karbala by God well before the event took place: (1) before the birth of his grandson Hussain, (2) at his birth, and (3) after his birth. Prophet Muhammad made it clear that those who were going to murder his grandson would be damned by God and denied divine grace.

It is reported that when Hussain was born, the Prophet rushed to the house of his daughter Fatimah. The newborn was brought to him; the Prophet recited the *adhan* (first call to prayers) in his right ear and the *iqamah* (second call to prayers) in his left ear and then caressed him. A friend of Fatimah who

27

was present noticed that the Prophet was crying. "Why do you cry when he was born within the hour?" she inquired. "I cry because this son of mine will be murdered by a deviant faction of my nation. May God curse them and never give them my intercession," the Prophet said.

It is narrated from Umm Salma, the wife of the Prophet, that he said "An angel entered the house on me. . .and he said to me, 'this son of yours, Hussain, will be killed, and if you wish I can show you the soil from the earth where he will be killed.' Then he took out some red soil."[6]

The reason for Karbala

When Yazid son of Muawiyah was illegally appointed caliph of the Muslim nation by his father in 680 CE (60 AH), he sought to solidify his position by securing the allegiance of all the tribal chiefs and local leaders, which was the custom in those days.[7] He

---

6. *Musnad al-imam Ahmad*, vol. 6, p. 294.
7. They had already established a stronghold in Damascus, Syria, which was the capital of the Umayyad regime.

achieved this through bribery, intimidation, and nepotism. Yet when it came to the grandson of Prophet Muhammad, who was the most revered and respected personality, he knew there would be resistance. Hussain immediately refused to pay allegiance to such a despot and criminal, even under the threat of coercion, and instead proceeded towards Kufa, Iraq, whose people had pledged to support him against Yazid.

Yazid's plan against Hussain

Not wasting any time, Yazid sent a letter to his cousin and governor of Medina, Walid son of Utbah, commanding him to get the allegiance of Hussain and his companions, and if they refused, he was to execute them.

In the middle of the night, a messenger from Walid went to the Prophet's mosque to invite Hussain and his companions to the governor's court. Hussain, accompanied by thirty men, went to Walid who asked for his allegiance to Yazid. Hussain immediately realized how precarious the situation had become for him and understood that Yazid's men would not leave him until he complied with their demands. Hussain convinced Walid to adjourn until the morning so that the matter could be discussed in public. That night Hussain left Medina with his family and journeyed towards Mecca.

Hussain's will

Just prior to departing from Medina, Hussain was visited by his half-brother, Muhammad son of Hanafiyyah,[8] who advised him to avoid the swords of Yazid by leaving the area and traveling away from Iraq and Syria. However, Hussain knew that avoidance would not solve the problem of Umayyad injustice and tyranny that had taken root in the Islamic nation. So, remaining resolved on this course,

---

8. The son of Ali and Khawlah, daughter of Jafar son of Qays. Khawlah was from the women prisoners of the tribe of Hanifah. Ali married her after the death of the Prophet. Muhammad was born in Mecca in the year 21 AH and died in 81 AH. He was an exemplary figure known for his knowledge, graciousness, and bravery.

Hussain traveled to Mecca but not before leaving his final will to his brother. He wrote:

> Hussain bears witness that there is no god but God alone and that He has no partner and that Muhammad is His slave and messenger; he came with the truth from Him, and verily heaven is the truth and hellfire is the truth and the hour [of judgment] is approaching, there is no doubt, and verily God resurrects those who are in the graves.

> And I neither go out seeking joy nor to renounce the blessings [of God], nor seeking corruption nor as an oppressor. Surely, I went out for no other reason than to seek reform in the nation of my grandfather Muhammad. I want to enjoin good and forbid evil; I want to follow in the footsteps of my grandfather Muhammad and my father, Ali son of Abu Talib. Know (that) he who accepts me by accepting the truth of God is more deserving of the truth. As for those who reject [my proposition] then with them I will be patient until God judges between us with the truth, and He is the best of judges.

This is my will to you, O brother, and my success is from none other than Allah; it is He upon whom I depend, and it is to Him that I present my case.[9]

Hussain travels to Mecca

Hussain left for Mecca at the end of Rajab 60 AH (May 680 CE) where he spent the next few months with the intention of performing the pilgrimage. In Mecca, he held a conference to rally support among the local Muslims and received over twelve thousand letters of support from Kufa alone. Thus, Hussain sent his cousin, Muslim son of Aqil, to Kufa to confirm the allegiance of all those who had corresponded with him. Hussain stayed in Mecca from the month of Ramadan (June) until the eighth day of Dhu al-Hijjah (September 9) when he finally decided to forego the pilgrimage and instead depart for Kufa out of fear of assassination.

---

9. *Manaqib ibn Shahr Ashub*, vol. 4, p. 88. Al-Bahrani, *Maqtal al-awalim*, 54. *Maqtal al-khawarizmi*, vol. 1, p. 189.

Muslim son of Aqil in Kufa

In the meantime, Muslim son of Aqil, Hussain's cousin and emissary, arrived in Kufa three days before the end of Shawwal (August 1). Everyone who had written letters of support and wanted to pledge allegiance to Hussain began gathering and organizing their activities. Muslim was able to collect eighteen thousand signatures of allegiance to Hussain and sent a letter to inform him to hurry to Kufa.

Word of Muslim's successes in Kufa reached Yazid and, fearing an uprising, he decided to replace the then inept and weak governor with someone who would crush the impending rebellion. He consolidated the governorship of Basra with Kufa by appointing Ubaydullah son of Ziyad, the governor of Basra, over both towns and commanded him to travel to Kufa to replace the current governor, seize control, and quash the rebellion.

Ubaydullah's cunning plan

Ubaydullah quickly realized that most of the Kufans were with Hussain and very few of them were with

Yazid. He cunningly implanted his spies and mercenaries to instill fear and persuade them to retract their allegiance to Hussain. He also placed a high bounty on the head of Muslim, and not long after doing so, Muslim son of Aqil was left alone to fend for himself in the streets of Kufa as the police searched for him. Muslim son of Aqil, along with a few sincere Kufan supporters, was finally detained and executed in the palace of Ubaydullah.

Hussain travels toward Kufa

On the eighth day of Dhu al-Hijjah, 60 AH (September 9, 679 CE), Hussain left Mecca for Kufa. He remarked, "I am leaving so that blood is not spilled in the Sacred Mosque (defiling its sanctity)." Along the way, Hussain received several messages and updates describing the status of his support in Kufa and finally the sad news of his cousin's execution. By then, Hussain was already in Iraq and so inevitably began preparing his caravan of family and companions for the difficult outcome that awaited them.

As he continued his journey, he was met by a thousand of Ubaydullah's men led by Hurr al-Riyahi who prevented him from going any farther towards Kufa or even from returning to Medina. Instead, Hurr was commanded to force Hussain into the desert area outside of Kufa.

Hussain arrives in Karbala

Hurr was commanded to be harsh with the caravan and prevent them from obtaining water. This forced the caravan of Hussain, filled with women and children, to finally stop and set up camp in a land known as Karbala, which was near the banks of the Euphrates River and about fifty miles (seventy-five kilometers) from Kufa. It was the second day of Muharram, 61 AH (October 2, 680 CE).

Hurr received orders to prevent Hussain from reaching the Euphrates, and in support of this, Ubaydullah also posted five hundred men at its banks. On the seventh day of Muharram (October 7), Abbas son of Ali, a half-brother of Hussain, tried to get water for the camp but was prevented from reaching it. Hussain asked the men to dig for water within and around their camp to find water so they would be able to drink. By the ninth day, the wells had dried up and whatever small quantity of water that had been found had completely run out.

The tenth day of Muharram

On the tenth of Muharram (October 10), Ubaydullah ordered his men to attack the camp of Hussain. Yazid had assembled an army of approximately thirty thousand men to fight him and his companions, who numbered seventy-three in total. The men in the camp of Hussain now knew that they would all be martyred.

The battle was initiated by Yazid's army who assaulted Hussain's camp with arrows, swords, and spears. They were met by his companions who went out valiantly to the battlefield, refusing to allow any harm to come to the grandson of the Prophet.

Among them were some like Hurr who, until that morning, were on the opposite side. From the period of stopping in Karbala to the tenth day when fighting began, Hurr was growing increasingly restless. He, and other conscientious soldiers like him in Yazid's army, could hear the cries of the thirsty children from Hussain's camp while bucket upon bucket of water was being given to Yazid's soldiers' horses. He knew who the personality was on the other side and who his mother, father, and grandfather were. Finally, Hurr said to himself, "Surely, I am choosing between heaven and hell. Verily, I choose heaven!" and joined Hussain's ranks.

Consequently, Hurr was the first among the companions to go out into the battlefield and be martyred. Then, one by one, each companion was martyred on the land of Karbala, either by repeated strikes of the enemies' swords, the deep wounds inflicted by the spears, or by the arrows that they willingly chose to shield Hussain from, until all were but scattered bodies on the battlefield.

The young men of the Holy Household of the Prophet are martyred

The men of the Prophet's family then entered the battlefield. Abbas and the other half-brothers of Hussain, who were the sons of Ali and Ummul Banin,[10] were martyred on that day along with the teenage son of Hussain who was said to have a striking resemblance to Prophet Muhammad. In addition, the son of Hasan (Hussain's older brother), who represented his father on that day, and the son of Hussain's sister Zaynab were martyred at the tender ages of twelve and eleven, respectively. Abbas, Hussain's flag bearer, was one of the last who remained alive next to Hussain. He was martyred on the way back from fetching water for the women and children of the camp. The bloodthirsty and wicked army of Yazid did not even spare the life of Hussain's six-month-old son who was shot with an arrow while his father was trying to find him some water in the hot desert of Karbala.

---

10. Ummul Banin was married to Ali after his first wife, Fatimah, died in 11 AH.

Hussain's valiant final stand

Hussain was now left all alone. He bid farewell to the women and then visited his remaining son, Ali al-Sajjad (Ali, the prostrating one), who was too sick to fight. His sister, Zaynab, brought him his horse and smelled his neck and kissed him on his chest, just as their mother (Fatimah) had told her to do before she died. She then sent him out to the battlefield.

Hussain was a valiant and courageous warrior who had been defending Islam and the truth alongside his father and brother. After killing many men, the enemy forces retreated so the archers could target him. Suddenly, the skies became dark from the arrows that rained down on him. The historical reports say the body of Hussain looked like a porcupine with the tails of the arrows sticking out from all sides. He was finally struck with a poisoned, three-pronged arrow in his chest, and the enemy immediately surrounded him and began striking him from all sides—they attacked him with their spears and swords, and he fell to the ground.

Unsure if he was dead, some of the enemy soldiers stormed the camp, set the tents on fire, and terrorized the women and children. Hussain, in his final moments, called out to the enemy to have shame as he tried to get up and protect the women and children, but he would fall to the ground once more.

Some of the enemy soldiers were hesitant to finally take the life of Hussain—after all, they knew he was the grandson of Prophet Muhammad—until finally one evil lieutenant came toward Hussain, who was prostrate on the ground, kicked him with his metal boots, sat on his chest, grabbed his beard, raised his chin, and struck his neck, cutting off his head. This is what the Day of Ashura, or the tenth of Muharram, is known for!

The orders from Yazid were to cut all the heads from the bodies and bring them back as trophies. The enemy soldiers severed the heads of all the martyrs, mounted them on the tips of the spears, and displayed them for all to see as the army returned to Kufa and later Damascus.

Prisoners of war

The possessions of the women and children, among whom were Zaynab and Umm Kulthum, the sisters of Hussain, were looted—even the earrings were snatched directly from the ears of the little girls, including Hussain's three-year old daughter. The women and children were gathered with Ali al-Sajjad,[11] who was in a very sickly state, tied with ropes one to the other with chains around their necks, and taken to Kufa to the palace of Ubaydullah son of Ziyad.

Zaynab and Umm Kulthum speak out

In any military battle, the laws of engagement and, indeed, basic decency demand that civilians be treated humanely. Even upon defeating an opponent, the victor must respect the sanctity and dignity of each human life and inviolability of personal property. After the event of Karbala, this consideration was not given to the captives from

---

11. Son of Hussain and next imam who survived Karbala because he was too ill to fight.

Hussain's camp. They were beaten, terrorized, and humiliated—first in the streets of Kufa and the court of Ubaydullah and then in Damascus in the court of Yazid.

Yet, history has repeatedly shown that despite what appears to be a crushing defeat, the truth is never eradicated. Instead, it persists and perseveres through the vocal protests and demonstrations of those who refuse to allow such a tragedy to defeat and subdue them. This was the case with Hussain's sisters, Zaynab and Umm Kulthum, who refused to remain silent and continuously spoke out against their assailants and the injustices done to their brother, their family, and indeed the religion of Islam.

In the streets of Damascus

After a brief period of captivity in Kufa, the prisoners were made to trudge through the desert towards Damascus. They were forced to walk through the

streets of Damascus on the first day of Safar,[12] 61 AH
(October 31, 680 CE). The people of Damascus
celebrated with beating drums, trumpets, joy, and
laughter directed specifically to inflict further pain
upon the captives.

---

12. The second month in the Islamic calendar which comes
right after Muharram

Chapter 6
The Umayyads Exposed

Yazid declares achievement of his revenge for the Umayyads

According to prominent Muslim scholars, Yazid was not a true Muslim, nor was he moral in any way. This is because he openly violated the laws of Islam and basic human decency in order to hoard wealth, secure power, and achieve revenge for the defeats his family faced at the hands of Prophet Muhammad and the Muslims in the early days of Islam. During those days, Yazid's father, grandfather, and uncles were pagans who not only persecuted and terrorized Muslims but also hunted them down to kill them. Some of those uncles and other relatives were killed by Ali when the pagans attacked and were defeated by the Muslims at the Battle of Badr in 624 CE (2 AH).

Losses like these, which were a result of their (i.e., the Umayyads) continuous attacks on Muslims and their own deep hatred of Islam and the Prophet's family, only further fueled the flames of revenge in their hearts. Thus, they pretended to accept Islam, or at least its inevitability, but secretly continued to harbor their ill will towards the Prophet and his family. Eventually, Karbala was a result of this scheming and planning which had taken years to enact.

The court of Yazid

The captives arrived in Damascus to fanfare and celebration, the likes of which only occur on great joyous occasions, and they were herded to the court of Yazid. The court was in full attendance, and Yazid mocked, ridiculed, and hurled insults upon Hussain and the family of the Prophet. Ali al-Sajjad fearlessly defended his father from Yazid's verbal attacks and requested that he allow him to address those present from the pulpit. Yazid reluctantly agreed, admitting that Ali al-Sajjad was from a family known for their knowledge and eloquence. Indeed, he eventually regretted that he did because Ali al-Sajjad's words shook the hearts of the crowd and brought tears to their eyes. He identified himself to the people as the grandson of the Prophet and the son of the Lion of God (Ali son of Abu Talib), the son of he who fought with the Prophet of God at Badr and Hunayn, the son of Fatimah and Khadijah (his grandmother) and the son of he who was drenched in his own blood in the land of Karbala (Hussain).

His words caused Yazid to tremble with fear—the people began to turn against him. To immediately silence Ali al-Sajjad, Yazid commanded the court announcer to perform the adhan (call to prayer). As soon as the announcer recited "I bear witness that Muhammad is the messenger of God," Ali al-Sajjad asked Yazid, "This endeared messenger, is he your grandfather or mine? If you were to say that he is your grandfather, then everyone will know that you are a liar, and if you were to say no, then I would ask you, 'Why did you kill my father out of oppression and enmity, stealing his wealth, and taking his women prisoners?' If my grandfather is your opposition, then hell will be your abode on the Day of Judgement."

Yazid ordered the head of Hussain to be brought into the court and placed before him on a golden tray in plain view of the women and children of the Holy Household of the Prophet of God. Such was his cruelty! Yazid did everything he could to inflict pain upon the captives and humiliate them.

According to some historians, Caesar's messenger was also in the court of Yazid. He said, "In one of our islands we have a hoof print of the donkey that Jesus rode, and we make a pilgrimage to it annually from all places. . .and we consider it sacred just as you consider your book sacred. Yet, I am aghast to stand here and witness you defile the family of your prophet; you are clearly in falsehood." Yazid's fury grew, and he ordered the Roman messenger be executed. The messenger kissed the head of Hussain and pronounced his statement of faith in Islam before he was executed.

Frustrated and defiant, Yazid ordered that the head of Hussain be hung at the door of the palace for three days and the other heads be placed at the gates of Damascus and the Umayyad mosque.

Zaynab responds to Yazid

Amid that pain and suffering, one powerful voice rang out to ensure the sacrifice of her brother would never be forgotten. Zaynab stepped forward and boldly delivered her famous speech in which she exposed Yazid's treachery, criminal acts, and indecent treatment of the captives. Her speech caused great turmoil and instability for Yazid, and so he placed the captives in a dark prison for three days, away from all the residents of Damascus so that no one could hear her words.

Zaynab uses her knowledge and eloquence to respond to Yazid

Yazid feared an uprising from the effects of having Zaynab stay in Damascus longer, for her scathing remarks (from the prison windows) and her eloquent tongue stirred the hearts of people and caused them to question him. She refused to remain silent about the injustices committed by Yazid despite the threats and intimidation. An ordinary woman might have crumbled after witnessing the tragedy of Karbala, but she was the granddaughter of Prophet Muhammad, and so she accepted the responsibility of keeping her grandfather's message, and indeed that which her brother died fighting for, preserved and alive. It was due to this unrelenting vocal defiance of injustice and tyranny that Yazid finally ordered that the captives be released and escorted back to Medina.

According to historians, on the way back, Ali al-Sajjad brought back the decapitated heads, including Hussain's, so that they could be buried with the bodies.

The significance of Arbaeen

It was on the fortieth day after Ashura[13] (known as Arbaeen) that Ali al-Sajjad and the captives returned to Karbala and returned Hussain's head, along with the heads of the other martyrs, to the grave where his holy body lay.

---

13. The day when Hussain and the men of his camp were martyred

According to Islamic tradition, as reported by two companions of the Prophet, Abu Dharr al-Ghafari and Ibn Abbas, he said, "Surely the earth cries over the [deceased] believer for forty mornings."

This is the reason why millions of followers of the Holy Household of the Prophet of God travel to Karbala in an annual pilgrimage to visit their martyred imam (Hussain) and all of those who died alongside him from his family and his companions.

The caravan of the Holy Household reaches Medina

The family of Hussain remained in Karbala for three days before departing for Medina. The holy city of the Prophet was in great distress at the sight of the released captives, and the news of what happened in Karbala quickly spread, creating anger and resentment. Soon after, in a show of force, Yazid sent his armies to destroy the Kabah (in Mecca) and to pillage, loot, and plunder the Prophet's city. Yazid, the vile and heinous criminal, did not live long after his crimes. He died in 683 CE (64 AH) after some say he was thrown from his horse.

Conclusion

Many famous and notable personalities from history, like Mahatma Gandhi, Sir William Muir, and Edward Gibbon, have lauded Hussain and his stand for truth, justice, and human dignity. This is the case not only because his life was the pinnacle of courage, valor, and steadfastness but also because it was an example of how one man, with the support of a few loyal and sincere supporters, can defeat a tyrant, and that military might is not a prerequisite for the preservation of truth. In fact, deep faith and conviction, delivered with resolve, eloquence, and beauty can ensure that what is true remains timeless.

This can be witnessed every year and in every land on the day of Ashura, when Muslims weep and mourn the loss of Hussain as if it had only just occurred, or on the day of Arbaeen, the fortieth day after his martyrdom, when more than fifteen million people gather yearly in Karbala to pay homage to this great hero. We stand in awe of Hussain and those who fought on his side, and we declare that, even today, we are with those people who, like him, struggle against evil and tyranny for the loftiest ideals and the highest human character.

Editor's Note

Muslims will typically pronounce a short prayer ("peace be upon him and his family" or "peace be upon him or her") when mentioning Prophet Muhammad, a member of his family, or other prophets. These short prayers are sometimes called honorifics. They are represented as lowercase acronyms in parentheses after names, such as *pbuh&hp* for "peace be upon him and his progeny" and (*p*) for "peace be upon him or her."

We chose not to use honorifics in this booklet so as not to distract readers who may not be accustomed to this convention since this booklet is intended for readers who are not familiar with the subject matter.

If readers are familiar with this convention and wish to honor the prophets and members of Prophet Muhammad's family, of course they may do so for themselves while reading.